AMAZING
CHRISTMAS
Activity Book

Written by Violet Peto
Illustrated by Kathryn Selbert

ARCTURUS

ARCTURUS

This edition published in 2023 by Arcturus Publishing Limited
26/27 Bickels Yard, 151–153 Bermondsey Street,
London SE1 3HA

Illustrator: Kathryn Selbert
Author: Violet Peto
Designer: Amy McSimpson
Design Manager: Jessica Holliland
Managing Editor: Joe Harris

ISBN: 978-1-3988-3122-3
CH010918NT
Supplier 29, Date 0523, PI 00003558

Printed in China

FESTIVE FIESTA

How many candy canes can you spot at
the Holly Town Christmas pageant?

CHRISTMAS WRAPPING

These presents are all mixed up! How many gifts can you count in the jumble below?

SNOW BUNNIES

All of these snow bunnies look identical—apart
from one. Can you spot the odd one out?

FOREST FEAST

These animals are enjoying a magical Christmas banquet!
Can you spot eight differences between the two scenes?

WINTER WILDLIFE

The names of three festive plants are hidden in these letters.
Can you find them? Cross out all of the other letters.

J H A F M I S T L E T O E K J G H O L L Y L K I V Y K U Y F

NUTTY FOR NUTS

This squirrel is off to collect nuts from his winter store.
Can you help him remember the way?

FINISH

START

CHRISTMAS CRAFT

Can you spot the only Christmas card
that isn't part of a pair?

ON THE FIRST DAY OF CHRISTMAS ...

Match each partridge to their pear tree.
Use the clues in the pictures to help you.

FOOTPRINTS IN THE SNOW

These little mice are lost in the blizzard! Help them find their
way home by following the trail that adds up to 40.

ORIENDEERING

Which reindeer has the correct directions to get to Santa's grotto?
Each reindeer's route starts at the corner square nearest to them.
E4 means go east 4 squares, W5 means go west 5 squares, and so on.

A

E5, S2,
E1, S2,
W1

B

W4, S5,
W1, S2,
E3

C

E3, N2,
W3, N1,
E1

D

W4, N3,
E2, N2,
W3

N

W   E

S

12

BURROWING BUNNIES

These rabbits are collecting presents to go under the tree.
Guide them through their tunnels and count up the gifts as you go.
Which tunnel has the most presents?

DO YOU HEAR WHAT I HEAR?

Brighten up these carol singers with your pens and pencils.

MISSING MITTENS

Three kittens have lost their mittens. Can you help them find them? Which mitten belongs to each of them?

BUILDING A SNOWMAN

Connect the dots to bring a cheery Christmas snowman to life!

BUNNY-BOT BUILDER

This elf is confused! Which box of parts should he use to build a complete toy robot?

SANTA SETS OFF!

Santa is loading up his sleigh! Can you help him figure out how many of each present he needs to pack? The total for each row and column of presents is shown on the right and at the bottom. Write the number in the circles below.

WOODLAND WANDER

Help the squirrel find a way through the forest following the trees in the order shown.
You can move up, down, and across, but not diagonally.

START

FINISH

THE NUTCRACKER

Connect the dots to reveal the villain in this famous festive ballet.

REINDEER REWARDS

Which reindeer received carrots as a treat?
What treats did the other reindeer receive?

FUN IN THE SNOW

The forest creatures are having a snowball fight! How many snowballs have been thrown? How many are there in total?

FINAL DELIVERY

Can you help Santa find his way to the igloo to make his last delivery, then back home to Mrs. Claus? Don't follow routes with holes in the ice!

START

FINISH

WINTER WAXWING

Which silhouette exactly matches the picture
of the waxwing wrapping a present?

CHRISTMAS HAMPERS

This beaver is making Christmas hampers for all the families in Holly Town. Can you help him fill each hamper by completing the pattern of baked treats in each row?

SLIP AND SLIDE

Which puzzle pieces don't belong in the jigsaw?

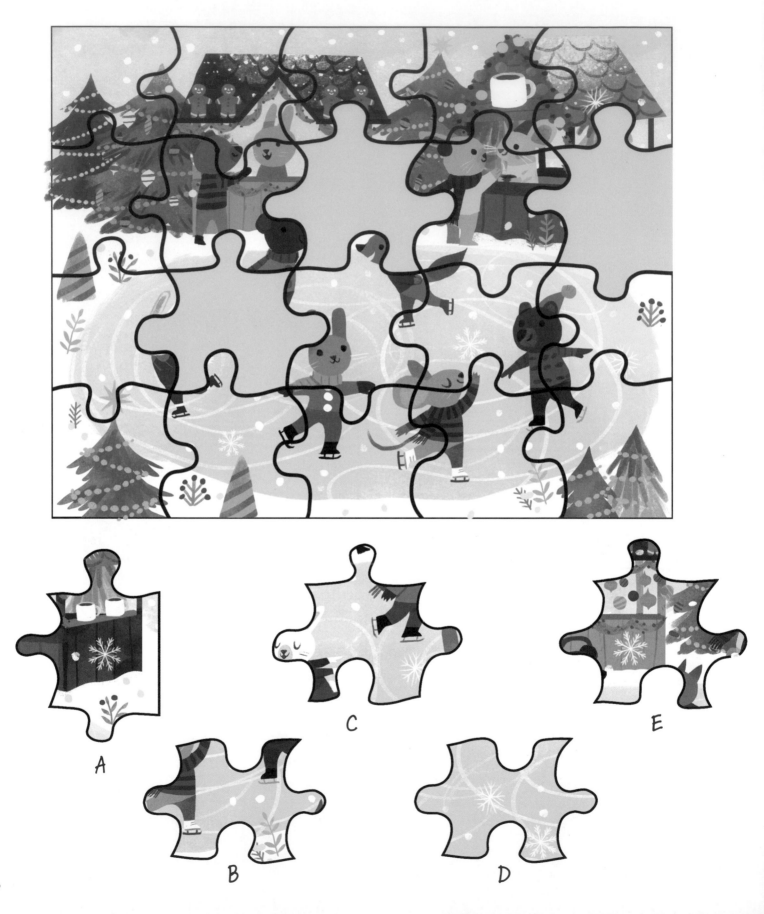

A

B

C

D

E

AND THE WINNER IS ...

These penguins love to race! Use the clues below
to figure out the order in which they finished.

The penguin in green finished four places behind the penguin in red.

The penguin in yellow finished two places
ahead of the green penguin.

The penguin in purple finished
ahead of the penguin in blue.

FINISH

WORKSHOP WONDERS

The elves are hard at work! Can you find each item from the panel in this scene of Santa's workshop?

29

STOCKING SEQUENCE

It's Christmas Eve and Mrs. Robin is hanging up stockings for Santa. Which socks from the basket should she hang in the spaces to complete the pattern?

WRONG ROCKING HORSE

One of these rocking horses isn't quite finished.
Which one is a tiny bit different?

PERFECT PIE

Help Mr. Squirrel complete the mixture for his famous Christmas pie.
Choose the correct path of ingredients by following the order shown.
You can move up, down, and across, but not diagonally.

START

FINISH

ALL WRAPPED UP

Solve the clues to discover who each present belongs to.
Write the correct names on the tags.

Micky Mole's gift is patterned with stars.

The wrapping on Oliver Owl's
present contains red.

The gift belonging to Frederique Fox does
not have a bow.

Kylie Kitten's present is not a vehicle .

Hitesh Hedgehog's gift has a yellow bow.

The wrapping on Gabriella Goat's
present is not patterned.

33

HOME SWEET HOME

Can you spot nine differences between these two gingerbread houses?

SANTA'S SLEIGH

Is it a bird? Is it a plane? No, it's Santa and his sleigh!
How many candy canes can you find?

GINGERBREAD BEARS

Use the clues below to match each gingerbread bear to its outfit.

The clothing with shoulder straps belongs to a bear in the top row.

The smallest bear's outfit is a dress.

The bear with brown eyes has patterns on its outfit.

The blue shorts belong to a bear with blue eyes.

ALL THE TRIMMINGS

Preparation is underway for the Holly Town Winter Ball.
Can you rearrange these panels to reveal the complete scene?

TOY TIME

Marvin and Myrtle are playing with their new train sets.
Calculate the total, from left to right on each train to find out
whose train is the fastest. The highest number wins!

$$12 + 18 \div 3 \qquad \times 11 \qquad =$$

$$17 - 5 \times 9 \qquad + 4 \qquad =$$

SANTA IN OZ

Santa is arriving in Queensland, Australia. Follow the clues to find out what the time and date it is there so Santa can change his watch.

It is 8:00pm on the 24th of December in Timbuktu.

Vancouver is 8 hours behind Timbuktu.

Mumbai is 13 and a half hours ahead of Vancouver.

Queensland is 4 and a half hours ahead of Mumbai.

CHRISTMAS PUDDING

Copy this picture of a yummy Christmas pud in the empty grid below.
Use the lines as a guide.

CHESTNUTS ROASTING

Which of the silhouettes exactly matches the
picture of the roasted chestnut vendor?

STARRY NIGHT

All of these stars are different, apart from a pair of twins. Can you spot the two that look the same?

CHIMNEY CHOICES

Which chimney should Santa choose to get to the stockings?

TOOL TIME

This elf wants to buy new tools for Santa's workshop.
Can you help her work out the value of each tool?
Write your answers in the circles at the bottom.

hammer × saw = 15

saw × wrench = 21

hammer × screw = 40

SPOT THE DOTS

These charming little houses all have dots on their roofs. How many dots should be painted on the houses that don't yet have any? Can you spot the patterns?

SANTA'S HAT

Santa has lost his hat! Can you help him find it?

Which of these snow geese is flying the wrong way?

FROSTY FUN

Can you figure out what the pattern is and then fill
in the white sled so it's sixth in the sequence?

50

BERRY CHRISTMAS!

Can you rearrange the squares of this picture so they form a festive wreath? Write the correct numbers in the empty grid to show where each square should go. The first few have been done for you.

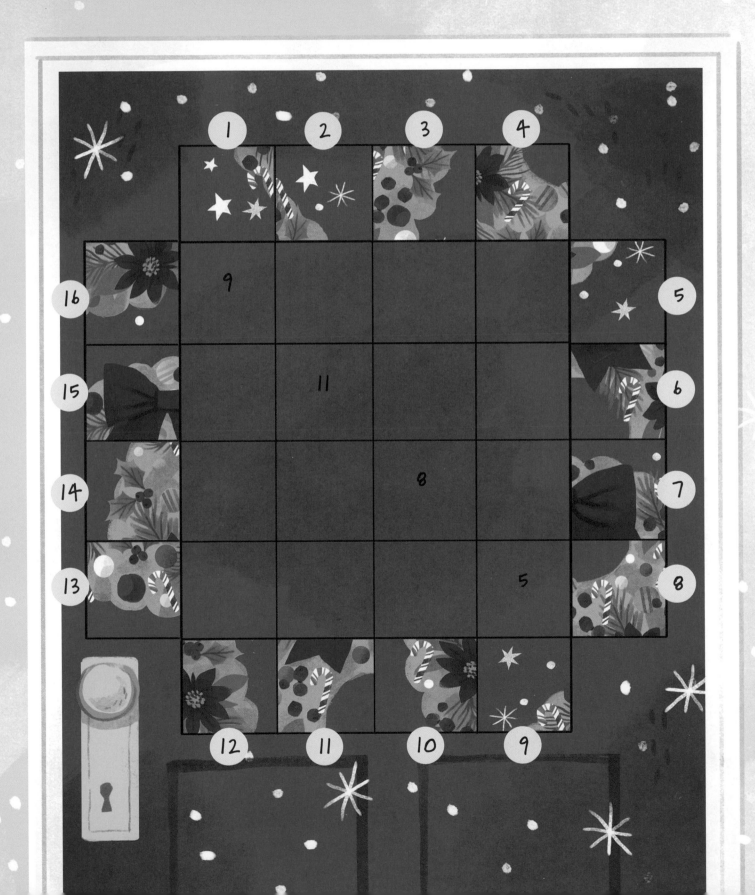

COOL SKATER

Which silhouette matches the pirouetting penguin?

CHRISTMAS CAROUSEL

Study this Christmassy scene and decide whether each
of the sentences below is true or false.

There are three horses on the carousel.

Mr. Cat is wearing glasses.

There is a blue car on the carousel.

There are nine lanterns.

There are six toffee apples.

JINGLE JUMBLE

How many bells can you count in this jumble below?

CHRISTMAS MORNING

These winter birds are celebrating Christmas with the dawn chorus!
Which tile is not part of the main picture?

MAKING MAGIC

These elves are making flying dust for Santa's sleigh. Help them measure out the ingredients and decide how many phoenix feathers are needed to balance the third set of scales.

REINDEER ROUNDUP

Help Santa check to make sure that all the reindeer are present and correct. Use the clues to name each one.

Donner has one brown ear and one white ear.

Vixen has an even number of speckles.

Cupid has a heart-shaped speckle.

Dasher has a white tail and a pink nose.

Dancer's hooves are mostly brown.

Blitzen has black hooves and a white tail.

Prancer has five-pronged antlers.

Comet is always jumping.

Rudolph has a red nose!

SWANNING ALONG

Can you count the cygnets in this river scene? If each swan has the same number of cygnets, how many cygnets belong to each swan?

CHRISTMAS SING-SONG

Can you rearrange the panels of this picture so they form a single scene of carol singers? Write the correct number order from left to right at the bottom.

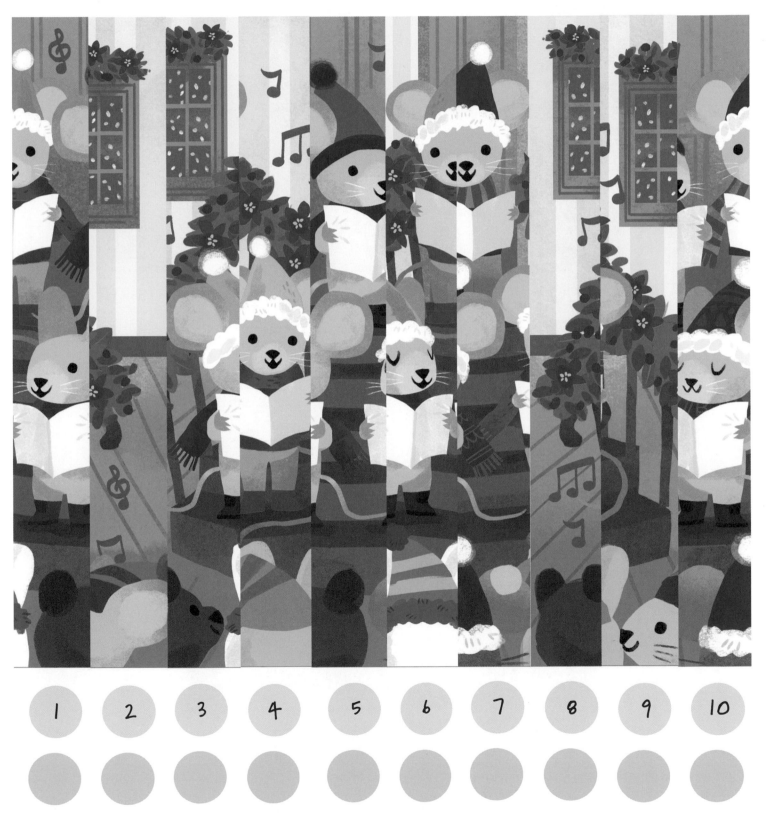

DECK THE DOORS

The residents of Holly Town have decorated their homes. Find out who lives where using the clues.

Ralph has decorated his home with paper chains.

Mildred has made a wreath with a red ribbon for her door.

Nina has made a festive frame for her door.

Carmen's house has two square windows and two Christmas trees.

Pierre's house has three round windows and a wreath with a yellow ribbon.

Adam has decorated his house with eight lanterns.

Oscar's house has round windows and six lanterns.

Shaheeda's house has round windows and a wreath without a ribbon.

SPARKLING SNOWFLAKES

It's starting to snow on this cold and frosty morning. How many
snowflakes can you count? Can you find the matching pair?

WINTER WARMER

Micky only wants pink marshmallows and Mona only wants white.
Who will get the most marshmallows in their hot chocolate?

SANTA TREATS

Connect the dots to find out what delicious treat has been left out for Santa. What message will you write to him?

Dear Santa

GINGERBREAD VILLAGE

Find each pair of gingerbread houses and use pens or crayons
to make the black and white one match its partner.

TOY TEASER

By looking at how these seesaws balance, can you figure out what arrangement of toys should be placed on the other side of the fourth seesaw: 1, 2, or 3?

LOCKED OUT

Santa has forgotten the code to get into the sled shed! Can you help? You need to place the numbers 1 to 4 once in every row, column, and minigrid.

FLIGHT PATH

Help Mr. Robin find a path through the blizzard to reach his family.
Which route should he take—red, green, yellow, or blue?

COOL RUNNINGS

These bobsledding bobcats have competed in a race. Using the clues below, can you figure out the order in which they finished?

The bobcat in a bath tub came after the competitor in the blue bobsled.

The smallest bobcat finished second to last.

The red bobsled beat the blue bobsled.

The bobcat with wings on her helmet finished between the blue and red bobsled.

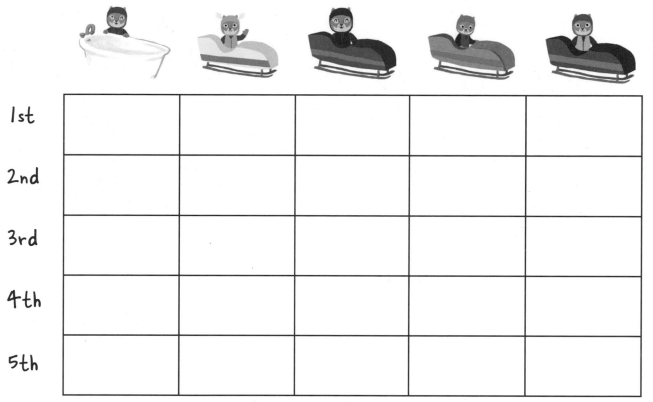

1st					
2nd					
3rd					
4th					
5th					

SAY CHEESE!

Santa and Mrs. Claus are posing with the elves for a team photograph. Which elf is wearing the wrong clothes?

GLACIER GUIDE

Guide these penguin explorers around the ice caves using the ladders and rope.
Plot the quickest route with compass directions. The first one has been done for you.
Beware: They cannot step in squares containing crevices or other obstacles.

N

W   E

S

DIRECTIONS

N6 ...

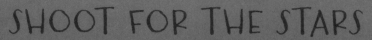

SHOOT FOR THE STARS

This owl wants to know which of the shooting stars is moving the quickest. Complete the calculations below to find out. Start with the number at the end of the tail and work your way forward. The shooting star with the highest number is the fastest.

$18 + 16 \div 2 \times 3 - 20 \times 2 =$

$5 \times 6 \div 2 \times 3 - 5 + 21 =$

$50 + 3 - 25 \times 3 + 9 - 30 =$

CHRISTMAS SHOW

These hedgehogs are getting ready to perform in the Christmas play. Can you help Whiskers, the wardrobe assistant finish dressing the performers? You need to find the correct three props for the snowman, Santa, and Rudolph costumes.

BIRD-OKU

Can you arrange all these winter birds in the grid so each bird appears once in every row, column, and minigrid?

SNOW STORM

Find a safe path through the storm for Santa by using the rainbows to jump over the lightning.

START

FINISH

MOUNTAIN MAYHEM

Can you spot ten differences between these two mountain scenes?

NIGHT FLIGHT

Look out, Santa—don't get caught on the spire! Copy this pretty picture in the empty grid below, using the lines as a guide.

TREE TEASER

Count how many there are of each of these decorations and decide which group cannot be divided by 3, 4, or 5.

SQUIRREL SKATERS

Can you find these groups of ice skaters on the frozen pond?
Each group appears just once.

SCUBA SANTA

Which route should Santa take to reach the beaver lodge?

PARTY TIME!

The Holly Town Winter Ball is in full swing!
Can you find each item from the panel on the right in this scene?

ANSWERS

There are 12 candy canes.

Page 3

There are 9 presents in the jumble.

Page 4

Page 5

Page 6

Page 7

Page 8

Page 9

Page 10

Trail C adds up to 40.

Page 11

Reindeer B has the correct directions to Santa's Grotto.

Page 12

Tunnel C has the most presents (18).

Page 13

Page 15

Page 16

Page 17

Page 18

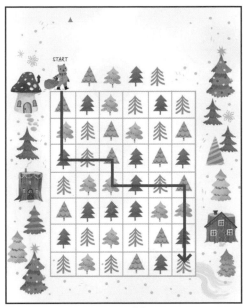

Page 19

Page 20

Reindeer A received carrots.

Reindeer B received hay.

Reindeer C received reindeer food.

Reindeer D received cookies.

Page 21

9 snowballs have been thrown. There are 18 snowballs in total.

Page 22

Page 23

Page 24

Page 25

B and D don't belong.

Page 26

The penguins finished in this order:

1st – Red

2nd – Purple

3rd – Yellow

4th – Blue

5th – Green

Page 27

Pages 28–29

Page 30

Page 31

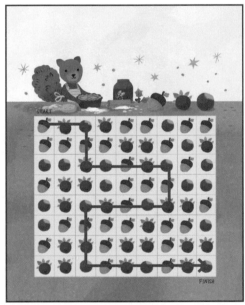

Page 32

Page 33

Pages 34–35

Page 36

Page 37

Page 38

Marvin's train totals 110.

Myrtle's train totals 112, so Myrtle's train is the fastest.

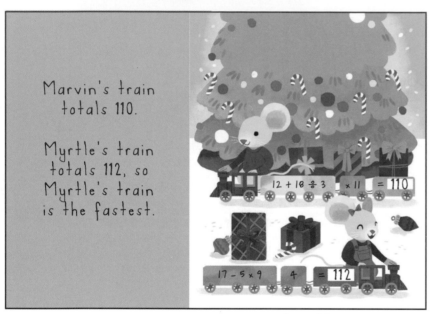

Page 39

It is 6:00am on December 25th in Queensland.

Page 40

Page 42

Page 43

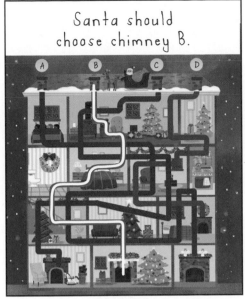

Santa should choose chimney B.

Page 44

X = 15

X = 21

X = 40

5 3 7 8

Page 45

2, 4, 6, 8
(add 2 each time)

A

12, 9, 6, 3
(subtract 3
each time)

B

16, 8, 4, 2
(divide each
number by 2)

C

D

24, 12, 6, 3
(divide each number by 2)

Page 46

Page 47

Pages 48-49

Page 50

Page 51

Page 52

There are 3 horses on the carousel. TRUE

Mr. Cat is wearing glasses. TRUE

There is a blue car on the carousel. FALSE—There is a green car on the carousel.

There are 9 lanterns. FALSE—there are 7 lanterns.

There are six toffee apples. TRUE

Page 53

There are 12 bells in the jumble.

Page 54

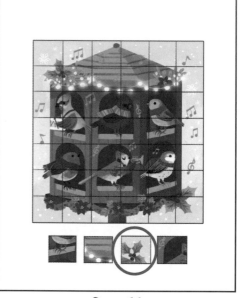

Page 55

1 crystal = 2 mushrooms.

1 phoenix feather = 2 crystals = 4 mushrooms.

So 8 mushrooms = 2 phoenix feathers.

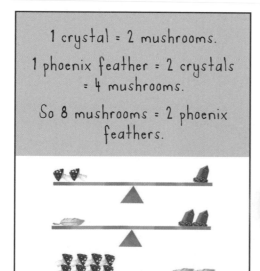

Page 56

Page 57

There are 9 cygnets and 3 swans. If each swan has the same number of cygnets, they have 3 cygnets each (9÷3=3).

Page 58

Page 59

Pages 60-61

There are 19 snowflakes in total.

Page 62

There are 11 pink marshmallows.

There are 9 white marshmallows.

Therefore, Mickey gets the most marshmallows in his hot chocolate.

Page 63

Page 64

Page 65

If a drum weighs 1, then a ball weighs 2, and a spinning top weighs 3.

So a drum, a ball, and a spinning top weigh 6 (1+2+3), or the same as 3 balls.

Page 66

2	3	1	4
1	4	2	3
4	1	3	2
3	2	4	1

Page 67

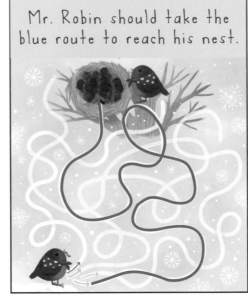

Mr. Robin should take the blue route to reach his nest.

Page 68

	1	2	3	4	5
1st	✗	✗	✓	✗	✗
2nd	✗	✓	✗	✗	✗
3rd	✗	✗	✗	✗	✓
4th	✗	✗	✗	✓	✗
5th	✓	✗	✗	✗	✗

Page 69

Page 70

DIRECTIONS
N6, E9, S4, W2, S2, E2

Page 71

$18 + 16 \div 2 \times 3 - 20 \times 2 = \ 62$

$\qquad 61$

$5 \times 6 \div 2 \times 3 - 5 + 21 = $

$50 + 3 - 25 \times 3 + 9 - 30 = \ 63$

Page 72

Page 73

Page 74

Page 75

Pages 76-77

17 cannot be divided by 3, 4, or 5.

Page 79

Page 80

Santa should pick route C to reach the beaver lodge.

Page 81

Pages 82–83